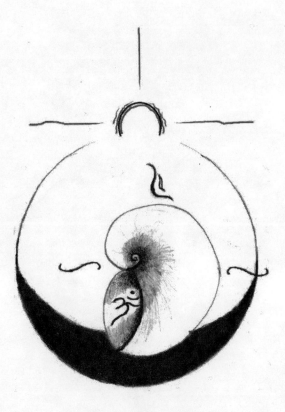

ISBN: 978-1494483210
First published in the United States by createspace.com. www.createspace.com

Temple

Joseph Montgomery

Preface

When we say the word "Temple", what image might come to the mind? Stone mason architecture, perhaps? Is there brick steeples and slanted rooftops? Elaborate altars and flower malas? Stained glass? Marble columns? A room clouded with incense? Ok, that's a good start... now we have a face... But what does a Temple mean? What is that word pointing toward?

Typically, these places are known for offering an earthly home to the gods. "Build it and they shall come—" structures offering a material abode to the energies we most adore. Shanti finds expression through the Temple filled with the people singing her names. Jesus gives insight to the man weeping at the altar. Support enters the life of the troubled who surround themselves with like-minded seekers. Universities are built for intellectual endeavors. Temples are designed for spiritual resonating.

A Temple is a body, or selected structure, for divine experience— a type of refuge for our spiritual efforts. It is a place to suspend our daily problems in order to connect to something higher than suffering. When we walk into a Temple, we remove our shoes and hats, these objects we wear to navigate in the world. Beliefs, opinions, speculations, obligations, we leave them on the mat at the door. We seek to reside in a Temple with bounding faith in ourselves and our relationship with something (anything!) Holy and Divine.

My thoughts on "Temple", and the reason for the title of this book, comes from the biggest realization that came to me in the process of writing these poems the past couple years. There really is no separate entity we must identify with to Be and feel connected. The essential Temple of Divine energy, the chosen location for holy breath, is and always has been—ourselves, in the daily, evolving Moment... it is our very own lives!

Our bodies are the ample cellular brick and mortar, the frame of slanted rooftops and bell-towers. Our minds drift of incense, the drum of worship, the blossoms of adornment, the strokes of art to invite the sacred. The lives we live are the expression, the relationship we cultivate with the Awesome Presence of Life. We need no other building outside of ourselves— We need only to move *inside* ourselves for the experience.

We are the original Garden for a life with God. Each of us a religion of our own Nature... Bow to everything— for everything, everyone, is a Temple for Love.

A Spiritual Living

Preface:

A Spiritual Living–

A characteristic of living with the modern, western-world mentality, is being faced everyday with a multitude of choices. We set out to find a simple tube of toothpaste and are faced with making a moral, educated choice between twenty varieties of brands (or more). We spend our days weeding our way through the possibilities— we make a decision with the hesitation that there could always be "better" choices elsewhere. Conventional wisdom says "be available to upgrade". We possess an association with *freedom* and having a surplus of *choices*— we believe we are free when we can have what we want... but this is a confusion. For Freedom is not about having everything we *want*— it has everything to do with being able to do what we *need*.

Truthfully, variety is an illusion of choice. We think we are free because we can reach out and grab whatever we like. But all this free-selection is actually demanding more energy from us, absorbing our attention with petty variations. The true choice we really possess, and must reclaim, is how much attention and energy we to give into something. True choice is married with consciousness— without awareness, it is compulsive reaction. Decision comes only when we know how much energy (attention) we are willing to give, and if we are willing to face the consequences, if our results do not come the way we intended... We face this dilemma constantly, in every choice, from breakfast to marriage.

The way we live spiritually is also a choice. It requires consideration of how much time and energy we're willing to give it. The brand of religion we pick isn't the issue. It is more about how much it means to us to ripen and evolve our personality for spirituality. It takes energy to be aware of these things. Some people choose to give nothing. Some, choose to give everything. Those who give everything are completely nurtured by spiritual excellence.

A common misconception of spiritual living is that it requires seclusion, renunciation from the world and its affairs... But for most of us, we are not called to go that way. For most, we need simply to choose the path of accepting our lives, where we stand, and moving forward from there. Increasing awareness of ourselves and the moment is the key. Spending our energy more consciously is powerful. A little discipline is the reins for bonding the driver to the horse. It's a relationship.

Living with discipline is not self-punishment. It is a conservation act. By withdrawing our attention and energy from smaller pleasures, we redirect that energy for use in more meaningful aspects of our lives. We forgo watching the television and use the saved time to play an instrument, sit down and connect with our spouse, chant mantra, or be quietly in prayer. We put energy into our higher qualities of life by sacrificing more immediate, sensual pleasures and securities. This technique continues refining into deeper patterns of the Mind, slowly offering a different perspective on Life.

Spiritual living is experimentation, discovering an optimal perspective for living. Life does not come easy all the time. It takes effort and a fair degree of integrity to pass through it. Our every action matters. Our every challenge is an opportunity. Our every interaction is a chance to understand. With this attitude, every experience is positively dripping with meaning. Our current situation will always pass. Change is a sure-thing to pivot our mentality on. What is really being asked of us, as human beings, is discovering (and putting into action) an optimal perspective and energy to manage what Life has in store for us.

And the way we do this is by making a choice— a continuously renewing choice to give something of ourselves and our days to the *practice* of deepening our approach to this Life.

A Game-show Miracle or Self-Realization?

Is this a Realization

or just another audition

for a pour paying gig?

So often

we talk about change,

but we return, still too impressed

by weary-old game-show marvels.

What is necessary for realizing

is to pick ourselves up

and participate

in our own lives.

Engage in the prizes

and the bankruptcies

with sincere

and alert

performance.

Automatically

we begin progressing.

Its not going to make any sense to you

at the start.

That's because our mind

is the King-debater.

Egoic Reason is the stick

for playing Ball.

The Heart is not a contestant

of that game-show.

It's just always there, centered

in great tides of winning

and losing.

Just notice who you are

and see if there is a longing

to evolve.

This isn't like an academic pursuit.

Its more like

a natural development.

This isn't a government handout.

It's like inheriting land

which requires consistent

and patient

conservation.

This isn't for everyone.

You don't have to

throw yourself into jeopardy

over paths to Self-Realization—

most of those

are just game-show miracles.

But If you suddenly

realize

that you are

walking—

then you're already

on the Path.

A Spiritual Living

Spiritual living

is like having my ear at a keyhole

listening

thinking myself holy

to have found the way

for knowing life's inmost secrets—

      Until

Existence opens the door

and I fall face-in

at its feet.

The keyhole, and I— Vanish.

Though we seek

with eagerness

and good intentions

we actually come alive

through our surrender—

putting surrender into action.

Because you see,

in order for the wick

to become

free

of the wax,

first we must

burn the candle.

Beware

If I borrow a bucket from the bathhouse

and clean myself outside

it does not mean I will smell

of those herbal formulas

which bathe Emperors.

    Because I have washed my feet

under the spout beside the orchard shed

does not mean I have plunged my roots

and begun bearing the weight

of summer plums.

A pack of coyotes

pick what they can stomach

from a bull carcass.

    Now they ramble into the valley

and say they are buffalo.

    This is not the way of initiation

into those light-pastures of contentment.

Beware of those dead bodies by the watering holes

who say to you

"give me your soul

and I will give you spiritual meaning."

Beware of those who say

"give me your Heart

and it will be protected by the nobility

of the scriptures I read."

Beware—

in fact

run like hell,

from those who say

"Follow me."

In the Question

Inside me

is a burning Truth

left unanswered.

I go looking for answers.

Everywhere around me

are unanswered truths

particles of the same

uninterrupted Question.

The Rain says to me on the roof,

"I have the Truth."

So I ask, "what is the Answer?!"

And the Rain

goes on raining...

Seeker

A Scientist knocked from outside

on the Cosmos

and heard that it was hollow—

A Lover of Life,

absorbed their attention Within

and heard themselves listening

to a music

as wide as silence.

Swimming the Experience of Water

When a fish has been introduced to its own fins

it begins swimming deeper

into the experience of water.

    That day the hawk first felt

the wind it could harness under its wings

meant it would give itself to the practice

every day thereafter.

Today I have discovered the propulsion

of Sadhana, when gathered

beneath unseen

passionately beating wings.

It lands us into arms that remember

the Moon is waiting

behind the rain.

Some connections

usher us away from fantasy,

bringing us back like a breath.

That's why if the opportunity comes

we need to catch the right attitudes

under our fins.

    Swim

courageously

through the waves cast by that pillar

which fell from around your head.

It may feel

at first

like drowning—

We may appear, for awhile,

like a piece of driftwood

pulled around by coastal waters.

But a time gradually comes when we land on the beach.

The waves touch us

but do not remove us.

It becomes easier

for more of our beautiful, rugged forms

to dive into those waves

playfully joining

some lean-hearted love-dolphins,

to explore together,

hug like lovers, and feel

the heart-beat of the ocean

drumming in the tides.

Experience the Self

Go inside and experience

the depth and wider

Self.

You

come out again

to ornament your Life

with the Reality you discovered.

The Show-Down

Inside this

Aching

lies a sexy

woman

and a lusty wish

for a high night dream.

Inside this

Capsule

lies a perfect image

fancy me saintly

with a beaten heart.

Inside this

Hand

is a promise

with interest

for a value of happiness

on the dotted line.

Under this

Tongue

rattles an avid

dispute

in tight defense of my side

of a small world.

Inside this

Head

is a power-house

Show-down

between a madness

and a beautiful mind...

But who's watching

the Show?

Genesis

The Myth is told

that God was alone

until he made Mankind—

So to solve his loneliness

he folded himself inside-out

from being the Godhead

into being Human.

Then he whispered to his human form, "The Fruit

on that Tree in the garden will take you further

away from Me."

Then God had the epiphany—

"Isn't that the whole idea of this madness?!"

So God gave Desire to the People

as Heaven's swiftest messenger.

The instruction was felt in the People

so they made a trade

under a fruit tree

with Kundalini in the blossoms.

The Serpent's offer

was to be full

with the power of God.

This isn't so

far fetched.

Humanity

just misunderstood

the deal.

They heard

"*I* can be as

powerful

as *God*".

The mistake in this

is that within Humanity's first thought

of themselves,

"I"

and

"God"

became two different

points of reference.

The original sin

was disunion.

But that was the splendid point!

To originate from the Source

but forget where we came from

in the game for knowledge

between Good, and Evil.

Now all of Life

can only be

one

or

the other

until we are free from dividing.

We have transmigrated

like Adam and Eve

from Eden Consciousness

to the Phenomenal Wilderness.

God sent himself further out

into his own Creation.

We are the Testament,

the Genesis,

but the Game is in the choosing

to experience the play

severing ourselves

into measures

of incalculable

beauty.

The Three Laws of the Universe

Birth.

Growth.

Destruction.

These are the Basics.

The unwritten Commandments

observable in every feature conceivable

in Life.

And these Truths

will always remain the basics

regardless how permanent

other rules of order seem to become.

Traditions and Religions,

Science and Philosophy,

Law

and Family—

these are all beautifully painted

road signs

along our way.

But in actuality

God

will never write down the Truth

in any One, solitary form.

If he did, then the stone

written upon,

the device who composed it,

and the language

used to say it,

would become bound under the conditions

of the Truth

they express—

They would do good work

for some period in time, but

eventually

they would die

or corrupt,

and we would certainly

forget.

God's truest solution

is to never stop,

never lag in the power

of showing us

the Truth in his creation

Every

Living

Moment.

Havan

When a child sees fire

for the first time

it sees only a light

it wishes to touch.

When it is burned

it continues to hold within itself

an ever-expanding respect

for the forms of Light

in Life.

    And Behold!

the first man to be bitten

by flames

was blessed also

with the wisdom to carry it

into his evolution.

    And see now

how far it has guided us.

Do not run from the discomfort, the labor

of growing.

That burning confusion is the call,

the natural selection

of Evolutionary fire.

Generosity of Flight

Spirit comes into a human being

and feathers our minds

towards wakefulness.

A shucked wing bone

may be useful in a kitchen

as a savory dish.

But try and fly with that wing

against the dawn colds

or through the tricks dusk can play

on your eyes.

You can't reach where the constellations abode

on nothing but the pluckings of theory

and a recipe

for success.

To be served the breakfast of princes,

sacrifice the feed trough.

Spend gold

if you want to experience richness.

Change your hording thoughts

into power,

devote power

into generosity,

and the effects will reach

beyond our world.

Then, open your wide wings over the earth

(an evolved shoulder catches less drag)

and dive into the valleys

of inspiring others.

See what it might be like

to engage in compassionate action

as though you are a falcon

launching from the forearm

of the Sun.

A New World Word

Preface

A New World Word—

There is an ancient Chinese curse: "May you live in interesting times." This speaks intuitively about the Age in which we are living. It has become impossible to pin-point, or to isolate the problem amongst us, for the situation is dramatically complicated by strife and unyielding selfishness. We are fragmented on almost every issue. But there is one thing we can almost all say together, regardless of your island of truth— we are all sensing something inherently dysfunctional with the way of the World. Everyone can *feel* the disheartened atmosphere of our societies. We strive for solutions. We remain confused. We must discover, for ourselves, an optimal perspective for living in the World...

We all have a role to play in the World, as it is. Spiritual life is no longer renunciation into caves and churches. It is not a blissful cloud we pull over our eyes, either. We need to find an evolved perspective for participating in this disjointed Civilization. From buying spices at the market to learning to love our spouse, we inherit truth which comes in forms of our daily living. We participate in our lives for developing mindfulness in the results of Life's endless situations. We begin to inherit Truth as we learn to observe our minds and reactions. Just as fire is inherent within the wood, so is Truth inherent inside of matter. But to access that fire of wisdom, it requires ignition, burning away the dense qualities of our minds and its fascination with matter, in order to unlock the heat and light— a less tangible phenomenon, but far more powerful.

The resources to evolve our civilizations are accessible. They are present. But we hold ourselves back from implementing our evolution out of fear of letting go of the techniques that have been successful for us in the past. The only way we can utilize and manage the advancements of our growth is if each and every citizen takes self-responsibility for the actions and thoughts that we contribute to the World. Our performances, and our phantasies, come with profound accountability to the whole mechanism of Life. Modern belief does not recognize this truth, but the very Universe shows us this wisdom in every way— and will continue teaching us, until it resorts to knocking us profoundly on the head, to wake us up.

Society *will* begin to speak a 'New Word'— a new form of civilization will emerge from the ashes of our ignorance. It will leave no space for old and tired dogmas— no insatiable egocentricity or attachments will survive in this new paradigm. Be patient— and brave. We must live with the growing pangs of a New World and accept the discomforts if we are going to begin speaking this New Word. We are obligated to the Knowing that springs from our Hearts... Think with your hearts, and we will surely move through these interesting times...

World Word up in Flames

The stars have lost their minds!

Raising and raining,

spinning

a contradancing wildfire.

Flaming arms are the tongues

loaded with wisdom

a word spoken

from this

cascading

Empire.

Burning also, was the pelvis heat

that melted this planet, once—

let it rest—

and then again, many more times,

kneading bread.

Bear in mind

you smoke-swallowers

light shines somewhere in those billows.

The spark comes

from deeper in.

A suggestion to you

pyro intellectuals—

burning your mind down

with another man's knowledge

can be useful

when it brings someone you love

with a bucket of water.

If it weakens your legs

get down on your knees.

If you're thirsty

lap up a river full of fish.

Drink until you yourself

are liquid—

a fish's breath.

Drown

inside a minnow's heart.

Dive

through a Heron's neck.

Fly into the mountains

and freeze

into snow.

Some seeds you crush

and their flavors blossom.

Some seeds you hide in the Earth

and their true nature rises up.

We burn through a forest

to awaken dormant saplings.

Spring will return

from the ashes.

Wake up!

The stars are burning!

A wind is coming

to carry the message

to the next watchtower.

Be Alone, Tall,

as a mountain spire.

Fortified by your awareness

you will hear the news

coming in on the air

the latest word saying

the world may be

going up in flames.

Jungle Mind

The Jungle Mind

in the deep bush

the jowls growling

monkeys howling

laughing at the serpent

who broke his jaw

to eat the bird's song.

The Jungle Mind

struck by money fire

burnt the bull elephant

smoking all the traces

sour business

for a profit, or perhaps

for a sure-thing.

The Jungle Mind

Hyped up the apes

got them ranting

the poacher's dogs

are panting, maybe for

a biscuit of meat

or a fuck in the kennel.

Blood of a Bengal Tiger

bones of a Heart King

for an expensive skin

rug for a Devil's den—

"What happened

to the Heart Emperor?"

The Spirit asked

the Jungle Prince.

"He was sold at a deal

for a ring

a rifle, and most

of all

a false sense

of righteousness."

"Was that wise?"

"No," he replied.

"It was a bargain."

Cheap Metal and Moisture

Doubt-thoughts are a wind

stealing moisture from travelers

on this long heartland pass.

Build Awareness

when it seems we are traversing unknown

desert rocks, filling ourselves with fatal imaginings

of how we might

                slip

and turn out a meal for the scorching sun

or some laughing dogs.

    When our souls are up

and mighty, a tent city

flapping like an ocean—

stay even more Aware!

    Uncertainty will come in through mice passages

and begin chewing on ropes.

Merchants come through the back

under the cover of reason

ready to sell us out.

Deceptive thoughts always arrive

mentioning the name of an old friend

we used to trust.

Why bother barking rhetoric

about the aromas of soul searching?

Who can understand the spectacular differences

between wood bark

and chocolate

when they intellectually abuse

any thoughts of sweetness?

There are many ways to lose

the moisture that keeps our basket flexible.

This kind of doubting

is a good wheel

spinning in sand.

You have a journey

to move on with.

Keep the lamp on

and do not sell the secret

to your flame

for coins we stamp out by the millions

on cheap metals.

In Motion with a Wagon

We are always moving into Changes

from some other point that is Ending.

A night sky pours from the glass,

finding our beloved's thighs in the endless

white sheets of our loving,

coming together

two hands in prayer.

Then we transition from this place.

Now birds are crying out for breakfast.

Sleep has hardened the ground

overnight.

We swing through the mundane

like a basket-handle at a farmer's market,

like a rough sack

at a grain mill.

Then we move again.

Someone drums a sermon on a Bible.

We send out emails to organize the crusade.

With all these soldiers at the door

you're adding more water to the soup.

And then we move—

The cumin seeds are smoking

in the butter.

Then again—

and we are taming a tornado

that dropped into a relationship.

Sadness... grief...

a stampede of doubt.

Next,

reciting poetry

like a drip of honey in the sweetness.

Then angry.

Then brilliant.

Then affectionate.

Then madness.

I see no end.

These are the passing of the spokes

on the great, mighty wheel

we're always beating

our heads against.

A World Word Song

The Word of the Universe

does not come by language.

However, when that mystical antelope

leaps through the heart-grove,

I will write about it.

When the river speaks

she sweeps a restaurant off the beach,

she cleans your hair.

A Baba sings to me

in rough tune,

and his song rolls on

the same cosmic floor

that pearled the earth

and these other necklace beads

around us.

Hashish is smoking, little pages

drifting, lips take it up

as life goes by.

Taste the wordless language.

I was once a dove

waiting up the sleeve of Jesus—

Now I am neither

the words of the prophecy

or the Prophet—

but I am a song of the same continent

where that visionary bird

flew in from.

Brothers of New Worlds

I remember

Brothers.

Brothers, we

use to crease the white paper

of our minds,

daring the System

that our realities are not

what they seem.

Perhaps the motivation being

to come out the other side

some part of us

an origami of truth,

and much of us

now edged for questioning.

I remember,

Brothers,

those glasses of water

shattering in our consciousness.

Many tides and many waves

in a droplet

on the tongue

to look deeply

and experience

from a different cup.

Behold, my Brothers

how ordinary our minds

tend to become.

I want you to know

I never felt small

in those experiences.

I forgot

a small part

of me existed.

Forgetfulness was a form

of a larger Surrender.

I imagined it was

the way an open flower

feels the world.

In these fluid moments

our evenings were music

in multiple dimensions,

a space we shared to hear

an audio spirit

beyond the ears.

Brothers,

it was never a high

but rather

a breakdown.

To dismantle persona

for a glimpse into the Self.

It was all

always short lived,

to exist that way, wide open—

and probably for the best,

because a fine line divides

insanity

from freedom.

Society could never understand

those landscapes of high planes

and what we saw there.

They could not accept

that divine absurdity.

An invisible boarder

drawls between reality

and hallucination—

we were pilgrims

further-stepping

into both regions.

A thin red line

defines breakdown

from surrender—

we were explorers

into both,

mapping new worlds

of Knowing.

I remember

You

my Brothers.

Boy

Love hurts the Heart

so it may grow—

Why, though,

does it grow so well on me?

A boy hides his Heart away

inside his imagination.

The lions on guard there

can become

any enormous size

of strength.

A pear was once bruised

and separated itself from the fruit

 bowl of brothers and sisters.

A cocoon split

and quickly got pecked

by some religious chicken.

A bell was rung in public

for the first time

and cracked.

He lent the candle he used for writing

to a person knocking

outside the window...

They used the word "borrow"

when they asked.

They used the words

"I promise".

But they never returned

with the wax of his good work.

That boy chose not to give light

to the blind anymore...

This boy's first lesson

of letting go

was to set free his first friendship—

the irony

that a turtle should run away

with his loving...

Friends became faster

after that,

but each one was given less

to get away with.

That boy learned

from his dog

what he didn't want—

A broken heart

one hundred times a day.

So he buried his love

in the sand and reeds

of an island he imagined by-himself

that he might push himself

into the distance

of an innocent sea of thought.

He wrote a beautiful poem

that day... It began:

"Love hurts the Heart

so it may grow—

Why, though,

why does it grow

so well on me?"

Lips on a Branch

These evocative politics I play

are flocks of domesticated parrots.

They talk

    but what could a parrot ever know

about speaking Truth?

I say things as though

I am God's open sea-lips.

Then something points

and I am shown only two mounds

of empty snail-shells.

The muddy tongue inside my mind

is talking with doubting waters.

I grow tired

thinking of my own opinions.

You stand below

wondering about this ripe fruit.

So many have come

to fill their blind baskets.

I am not the shade you seek.

I am merely one

leaf in the woodland

who will certainly, someday,

withdraw my feeding lips

from the branch.

The Opposite thing to a Diamond, is a Mouse

The opposite thing to a diamond

is a mouse.

A woman dances

wearing polished diamonds.

She is a star-spangled marvel

she is the party-night sky.

A prince is searching

for his one-hundredth wife.

So he begins combing diamonds

into his mustache.

When a diamond is in

the possession of a human

it becomes a public affair.

A mouse, however,

will never appreciate fame.

Even if it is prized

within a crystal cage

with a jade wheel,

if it escapes,

it will run to hide

inside the walls.

    A mouse in the presence of humans, is rarely

a pleasant affair.

They have talents

for scattering a dinner party

and making respectable men

leap onto tables.

    They would never

wish to be seen,

but prefer nesting

in the silent depths of a house.

    A diamond may never sleep

in the spot-light of adornment.

So outgoing

yet

afraid.

A man trains a vicious dog

to stand in front of the doorway.

No person can go in, the owner

cannot leave his house.

His wife sleeps with an expensive gun

hidden under her ear

loaded, even when they make love.

A mouse shoots across the room

when you're in the middle

of your most private

gestures.

We cannot hide

the fact

that things are being hidden.

We decorate ourselves

with objects that glamour—

but it will never cover up

the ways in which

fear

unravels us.

    You cannot conceal the mice

under karats of fashion

Likewise

you cannot wear a rodent

like you would

a ring.

Not More Flags

It is time to unravel

our obsessive preoccupation

with

Flags.

If we took the courage

to banish that seamstress

who continues printing the images

we cling to—

what will remain afterwards

will be nothing more than threads

flying into the wind...

Fear has a similar flag

as War—

When we begin to contemplate this,

we see,

we do not ever know

who really hurled the first thought

of oppression.

How can we truly sketch out

who our enemies are

without eventually realizing

our own hand at work?

We are told about good-guys

and bad-guys,

but no matter whose dog

we choose to feed

we feed

the fighting.

The proportions of fear are like those

of a war. We do not see

the dimensions which define it,

however, across the globe

we can all taste blood

in the drinking water.

If we're ever going make light

suitable for breaking through

the fire-power of a human mind—

then we need to develop

a way to do the work

inside us

before we condemn the situation

outside us.

We need to understand the consequences

of being Ourselves.

Give understanding a chance.

Not more Flags.

Radiant Forecasting

The pissing of the rain

through the fowls of wind

is a feeling in your Mind.

The weight of thunderheads

draped above your senses

is your own

veranda of fear.

Try speaking a new word.

Soon day makes the night clear-off.

Clouds are easily broken, when it's time.

Sometimes fog moves-in

above our Sunday-afternoon plans.

Sometimes rain predicted to

comb over the mountains

winds up crossing the sea instead.

Is this because the Sky is unintelligent

and confused?

Or could it be that Life's weather is

not a matter of instruments

and calendars?

Observe the way light blooms

through the tail of a storm-front...

Is that merely a heavenly photograph?

Or is it a more unspeakable

telling of design

behind Life's

radiant forecasting?

The Good Wait

A journey ends, another

seamlessly begins.

I have not yet wept

for all that I have seen.

Where have those tears gone?

    I have not yet told the story

the way I remember it.

What will happen to the memories?

Opened and flushed

I've come back from that sweet

rough love-making.

O how Life has turned me

on and on

and on

in her bed.

She has sent me back

to the end

I left behind.

Potential now

for starting a new

beginning.

All of these affairs in the world

these burning problems

that are all flame

and no light.

Can we change the focus?

"But if we do not have our worries

digging out our graves,

what will we have

to weep for?"

I understand...

But the tears we truly seek

come from the purifying grief

of profound gratitude.

To Know

that we can

Love.

The Heart splits like a wave

across that rock.

I am waiting on the tears

for all that I have seen.

Patiently working

smoothing a stone

at the salt-tides and

weeping sea

of my beloved Heart.

Between Oceans Apart

It is a long, deep breath

between the World

of the Metropolis

and the untouched

Misty-Hearted Mountains.

A Man of Spirit—

A Woman of Soul,

they are the only

who know.

Who are subtle enough

to zephyr that path

between both.

I am thankful

that there is a shore

inside us

unbeachable

by this world's

armor-clad profiteers.

Their smoky cannons

are their minds.

Their wars

are their creations.

I am calling for

that pure direction

where I am the Vessel

with godspeed sails

and a forest for a body.

Undivided

between the rising

and the setting

horizons.

I am here

seeking that clear breath

between kingdoms.

Where to worship Silence

on the most transcendent mountain,

yet trade my Art-of-Living

in the commerce

of the people.

I am here

for that long, deep breath

between the City of Men

and the Heart of Heaven.

A Man of Spirit—

A Woman of Soul,

they are the oceans with their tides

reaching to hold

the breast of those two coasts.

A Loving Friendship

Preface

A Loving Friendship—

It happens in Life, when we experience a relationship with another person that spontaneously ignites loving changes within us. Sometimes they come in the scenario of a spectacular romance, or perhaps, a steady and meaningful marriage. It may express itself in a friendship, a business partner, or a teacher. It could spring from two talents starting a band together, from a chance connection under the smoking veranda, or a mystical encounter with a spiritual personality. The scenarios are endless— and each time the story is worth telling.

These experiences tend to rise out of our consciousness with palpable generosity. We tend to go through the whole spectrum of emotion. Our minds spin into dizzying arguments with itself to "explain" what is happening. The dreams we have used to architect our identities suddenly turn back into wet mortar. Unexplainable things begin happening. A wall falls down. We weep. But now our house has just been joined onto another good house. We slowly expand this way.

This is not a situation in which one asks, "what do I get out of this?" We may ask ourselves that for awhile— but eventually it feels like dead weight. Like someone in a life-threatening situation, we start dropping the excess without much thought afterwards. This skin-shedding happens again and again, and we give it, because our thoughts are gradually shifting toward the happiness and growth of the Friendship, rather than either person's own ego. We are pulled toward a face within our lover.

We spend hours in conversation with a person because we hear a music within them. We endure the confusion and insecurity— our perspective shifts, and now these uncomfortable episodes become enduring moments of cleansing.

Follow that inner mysterious curiosity. The path of following the Heart is a strange, nonsensical unfolding. It becomes less about choice and more about allowing this weird and fulfilling life to wash over us, as it comes, in waves of loving friendships.

Big Heart Sun

I can't seem to stop

talking about the Heart.

It has dropped me like a teabag

into another pot for cooking

with mountain water.

So I won't jump out,

it turns the heat up

slowly.

Does that lead us to the conclusion

not to trust the Heart

with the temperature of our bathwater?

Before you answer, notice this:

how one cup of tea

from that kitchen

fills the house

top to bottom

like a whole shipment

of chamomile from China.

One loose leaf

which you cut with unquestionable

tenderness,

you cut

and stored

as your only link

back to the Sun.

But the garden was already

grown through your hair.

The whole day

already rose

across your forehead.

Just get to work

amongst the tea-leaves.

They can't seem to stop

talking about

the Big

Heart

Sun.

Over a Meal of Love

A rose bush spreads and falls open

As a boy hands a girl

A flower.

Two sweethearts feed each other

The strawberries of their minds.

They speak together

About the meal of Love

Together sharing

In the unfolding clementine

Of the unspoken.

Her skin was a milk

He stirred into his tea.

His lips were a slice of red fruit.

Bravely they held each other's hand

As slowly they dipped

Their senses into honey.

As gradually they tasted

The tahini of their Hearts.

Many things

Were awaiting their return—

The discipline of the ashram

Waiting cross-legged on the floor.

The state of responsibility

In front of documents

With their names printed on them.

Expectations and performances,

Community space and the gravity of duty.

Yes, many things

Anticipated their balancing acts.

But on this afternoon

A rose bush trembled

As it poured open.

A pearl was seen out of its shell.

Conversation took place

Over the meal of Love,

As a girl so lovingly

Smelled a flower.

While Feeling and Fire

Somehow, my dear,

you set a fire

subtly to me—

It is happening

    that I am a brushpile

of beautiful night-moths

      and aggravated scorpions

being raised from their sleeping.

This fishbone in

my throat   now

    wants to start singing.

My heart apple has asked

to merge

with your deer body—

then perhaps a promise lies within us

that a blossom will be created

from the seeds we sow.

    I do not know

so much

    about the way I feel toward you—

I have only observed in your face

is a whisper of the name

I should sing to open the heart-cupboard

    inside me.

I do not understand

    so much

about how this is

suppose to happen—

but I have played

the unlovable

    with great strength.

Now something gives way

and I am composing poetry

with love

beside the fire in my mind.

Yawning Wings

I will confess

to this page,

and to you,

that my love-wings

are soft

and know only their width

because I have stretched them

yawning in the nest.

Yet it is happening now, my love,

that I am becoming aware

of a sky.

This fragrant mind,

these heart-thoughts,

incubate

for that endless blue yonder.

Here I am confessing to you

sweet form

of my thoughts

that these love-wings

have not yet crossed a body of water

like yours.

However,

something inside me,

abounding me,

knows your winds

through their feeling

and has made me aware

of skies much higher

than where I stand

today...

Mouth that Heals

You were a soft itch,

and I

a loaded fire.

Neither could be ignored.

We stood near each other

without touching

but caring

with one thousand nursing hands.

Then the time eventually came

when we were ready.

The sky pulled down

to give us privacy, to make us

a secret

one hundred booming kings

scatter their gem-stones to know.

My gratefulness is a high spring garden

where lords come for prayer

and princes kneel

to sacrifice play-boy love

for the heart breaking-open

of manhood.

If we find a woman

whose loving is a teaching,

she becomes a garden

or place in the forest

that shows moonlight to us

in a whole new way.

Her body is a bough of fruit

her ripeness will invite you.

The light of the Sun lies with the field

and whispers gently into its ear.

Bring me into that perfect communication

with You.

Bring me into that flesh-communion

like the thorn

and the torn shirt—

the slight lift of blood

and the joining of

the cut

to the mouth that heals.

Reaping the Sweet

When something shakes the flower bush

an aroma deeper than the pain

drafts into knowing.

It speaks,

"don't weep for the blood

pulled by the sharp branch.

Weep, because in the sorrow

tears are the blossoms

leading the way

for the fruit.

A sign of the reaping."

But don't send the pickers out yet!

Mature the longing.

Those tears eventually lead to celebration!

Then Friendships arrive, throwing off their tight shoes,

to carry in the grapes of the Land together.

    Cut the bread at *that* time, while it's still hot!

Bring out the butter

and slabs of full honeycomb, too!

Mundane Lovers

How does the mundane

cope with this Loving?

Two lovers pull a long white cloud

across their bodies

and the Universe between them

unlocks!

Time and duty

vanish.

Bliss is in their exploring fingers.

A freckle

calls out to God.

A tongue

touches the fire that drives nations

away from contentment

into conquering worlds, or building wonders.

It's all there.

The jackals of hunger

quiet their whining.

The mind is a bird

listening to the song of its mate.

They stare into each other's eyes

as if a star was born

from an eyelash.

Yet, like all plumes of light

and dust

gravity slowly gathers all things.

    All particles contain

their own duty to the whole.

The lovers must, once again,

draw back the curtains

and dress themselves as actors do

before their parts on stage.

A time to put into practice

playing the game of civilization.

The rhythm is still theirs

to play on harp-bodies.

To take with them

into the tap on brass cups

slap on the steel pails

of the market

street-music.

Shake a bag of chickpeas

and they remember their beloved

in a way

I cannot begin to describe.

Somehow her bartering for turmeric

completes the poem

he wrote on her body.

Pleasantries with the baker,

merchants hustling silk,

mounds of uncrushed pepper

or the dance of coins in exchange—

somehow all these

things

become to those who love

not what they seem to be—

but begin to join the Spirit

behind

all

we

Do.

Cutting Threads

A person follows a gold thread within them

and they discover

clips of fabric from God's

most intimate sleeve.

We fall in love with a patch.

A man finds love with a woman

and falls into confusion

trying to calculate the distance

between her collar and her ear.

He gets hung up thinking about

the button which closed her breasts

inside her shirt.

Meanwhile, her eyes

are saying everything.

Lovers throw off their clothes

and the people swarm the floor with scissors

cutting threads.

Look to the left,

to the right—

look all around...

Those hollow suits,

all these flowering saris,

that lost scarf,

all you see

is where Love exists.

That realization

is worth celebrating,

shedding our outfits

and embracing

in energetic

conversation.

Lapse in the Heavenly View

Inside this cup

I am sometimes full

other times, crescent

to the brim of your lips.

You drink,

and out of fear

I navigate abruptly

away from the winds of your loving.

I try to drive the stars out of my passage.

I wind up beaching myself somewhere outlandish

with jungle-cannibals wearing

the bones leftover from my hunger.

Now a thought is coming

which makes my teeth chatter—

Please have patience with me.

When my awareness is slipping

as if the Moon

were a leaking bath

I slowly grow dry

like breathing

with my mouth open.

Sometimes I become so hungry

there is no satisfaction left

on the Good Earth.

I start eating

with the cannibals—

Please have patience with me

when I am like this.

My face is a galaxy

passed over by a cloud.

Wait for me—

There is a lapse in the heavenly view,

but I will soon write poetry

once again

across your naked sky.

Mare-Heart Song

A thoroughbred is bound by the legs

but the knot

slowly begins slipping.

    Sunlight hints to a full pasture. Wind

combs the grasses for music.

The love of the Mare plays to that song

as the Stallion-heart of her lover

is far away being broken.

Loving moves the farmer's daughter,

to dance in her skirt

like a breath moves through a flute.

The maid brings warm cardamom milk,

but her lover is pouring

moonlight from his chest.

    Harvest-moon throws a rope to her

balcony tonight

and rises—

a new song.

The Mare cries to that same music

from the cornfields.

    It breaks each heart open

differently.

She goes in search, weeping.

Beyond the paddocks, wandering—

eventually bridled by gypsies

their food to her

is bristles of straw.

Husks

with no kernel...

    This life will never satisfy.

Her heart is longing too greatly

for the one who drives

wild stars and gods

into perfect circles through the night sky.

Eventually the Sun throws a rope

to the suffering—

and like the shepherd Joseph

in the bottom of his well

will rise

to a greater understanding.

This Phase of the Moon

This phase of the moon

is closing,

a slow, slow shutter.

Yesterday it was a wide opened eye,

a deep bellied basin.

Now a sharp sickle brings out the farm-hands

cutting down this grass for broom-making.

A few more of these cycles

and the apples will be ready.

However,

a cow hangs out

under the trees, eating

as they fall.

No one can keep the hog

out of the compost.

Listen to these images.

This is not just

a picture book.

Have you met the farmer's daughter?

She invited me over her body

the way the moon

pulls over its shadow.

Every food

has its right season.

Hallelujah

Hallelujah cried the trees

growing windswept across this Spirit coast.

There is a story about

A woman who came to visit a young man.

She stood with him lovingly, in the doorsill

like a mountain-range—

The man, he was

a bloated cloud

hanging-out over the sea.

She invited him to end his swirling

and come to land.

Her creek stones called out to him

for more water, for they

were not smooth enough yet.

Her vegetation were dry tongues

speaking a Name

they knew could heal.

So he found the courage

to join with her.

Blowing, throwing waves,

he flooded inland, crashed the beach,

and split open

against her peaks.

Imagine a family reunion

of people who love loving.

The feast table is set

for the whole extended family,

however,

only one large goblet

is offered around

for the wine.

Every lip

drinking on the same brim—

the laughter getting heavier

from the same cup.

That's how the rain-forest of her body

and her beautiful mind

opened their lips

to his rain of longings.

We are emptied

into perfect listening.

Filled again

with gratitude.

Something happens

between two natures that love—

Jubilee in the rain!

"How can I help you?" He asked the Mountains.

"Be the sky

that I might pitch myself against you, majestically,

in perfect proportion with the Earth...

How do I help you?"

"Let me flow over you

near that seam patching Earth

to Heaven.

Let me tip myself into the colors

mixed when you are ablaze

with yourself."

Hallelujah is a song of praise.

Lovers are the ears

and lovers are the lips

windblown

in that voice

singing of the Spirit.

So Shall This

My Desire has turned me on

to you, sweet one.

Yet I strive

to remember—

how forest fires

are not the way

for finding secret temples

in your nature.

My attraction has turned me on.

However, I strive

to remember—

all the earrings

in this sparkling empire

are not breadcrumbs leading

into the dazzle of the Soul.

I am sometimes

conflicted over you.

Yet I strive

to remember—

war has never been a way

for two hands to meet

and understand.

I feel an urge

to make love in you.

So I strive to remember—

how a mind of pistons

does not enter the deep earth

as intimately

as the roots

and the rains.

I find myself

believing in being your lover

like a thing forever lasting...

But then I remember

how grain after

grain,

the mountains

are washing away—

they change...

And so shall this.

So shall this.

Hand-made Coat

Love has come unto us, this hand-made coat,

hung on the curve of a soft hook, our loving.

A poignant hurt is a part of this— a needle

laid in the sleeve while sowing.

Beautiful Life drives it now,

as a mother seams boundless love

into small sizes,

winter clothes.

Stroking into my pulse, swimming

toward its source.

It goes deeper, believing

it is looking for you.

Because you have awakened me, further.

But Life only speaks the information

I need to hear.

The rest dissolves

into longing

and faith.

It believes you are looking for me,

but we both know

a weaving is at work

much greater at Knowing

than these two spinning threads

You and I.

When Lovers Find Eachother

When lovers find eachother

they have already begun a journey

to move through a curtain-land of dramas.

The shapes which form

there out of shadow and fabric

are the billowing of half-loves, the offcuts

of their loving.

The whole Love is the rope

they follow with their hands—

it leads them out,

it also leads them together.

You will find they may wrestle for the pace

but they cannot pull

against the rope.

Moments of long

soft grass comes to them.

They rest, using their fingers

to comb rags down

from each other's hair.

Love brings them into groves

of unexpected flowers—

then the rains come

gently to bring their personal wandering

under the same shelter,

 that they might share

in the same rough blanket.

Wanderlust

Entertainment

Faint-heartedness

are all just clouds

teasing them with rainy landscapes.

There is no mission.

The soul of Love

pours the robe patiently

from their bodies.

Love reveals lovers, that

they were always

necklace pearls

huddled closely to the neck, listening

for the voice of their Beloved.

When lovers meet

they have already begun a journey

to follow the rope and remember,

that wherever they are going,

they were there

when they found eachother.

A Mountain Wilding

Preface

A Mountain Wilding—

I was on a walk this morning in the forest as the snow began falling. The sun was rising and I was pushing this body above its lethargic mind in the grey wisdom of winter. With a deep sense of connection and respectful fear of Her magnitude, my mind was a muddy ground, but my heart was a sky burning with Her morning beauty. To be a drum for the hands of the Earth, I need not overthink it, because I am already penetrated completely by Her rhythms. All of Humanity and The World are absolutely absorbed into the energy of this Creation. Even our misuses of the environment and pollution of our livelihoods are the play of urges Nature has put forth inside us... Man or machine, technology or wildflowers, fossil-fuels or honey, it is all equally the wilding of the Earth, our Divine Mother.

It is our mistake in believing we are separate. Whether by religious superiority or ecological guilt, we hold ourselves away from these startling growing-pains of our species. My dear friends, we are *still* evolving, and we mustn't harden our minds around our situation. How do we learn to wield fire if it does not first show us the destruction of its flames? Either by burning down a house or scolding our hand, we must learn. The human mind is the evolutionary fire of our time— we are standing at a threshold. Humans must utilize a different energy for living if we are ever to discover a new way of thinking.

We are all Beings of this Universal Nature— it feeds us all. It is a rich, intelligent energy that has the capacity to ignite billions of stars and continue their gargantuan fire for eons. This force buckles space-time and brings gigantic systems closer together. It builds itself into ever higher plateaus, and then creates Heros to challenge it's own wondrous summits... and yet, to my humble amazement, it also boils tea for the weary, and it grows our fingernails. Politics, Family, Celebrity-faces— all of these things we dive our attention into, The Universal Energy creates all of these things, and much, much more that is far too bright, or too deep, for our senses to perceive.

Surely, my friends, all peoples of this planet can sit at this earthly table and sustain our lives of work from the fruits we all grow. Surely, we need not crave for more than we need. We need not distribute our progress amongst the homes of the few. What would life be, I often wonder, if we chose to understand our bread, instead of taking it?

Selfishness is the dominant instinct of the animal kingdom that is still with us from growth, and that holds us back. Humanity is beautiful and creative, but self-centered. We use our wondrous ingenuity for personal profit, holding back the gifts of Evolution from the rest of the species, causing huge divides between Peoples. Someday soon, just as agriculture arose to transcend difficulties of food-dependency, or just as Industry arose to conquer the difficulty of man-power— just as the spine grew to free the body from the restriction of gravity, so will something arise in our evolution to transcend the limitations of the Ego. Have Faith.

We have the opportunity to experience Life at greater depths than ever imagined.... Like the Earth, we can open our soil— feel the power inside us, invite Nature to reach in, cast us with light

and rain, and begin wilding the frontier of our Existence. Give
Evolution a chance.

Day and the Moon

The Sun rises quickly.

I get out of the way.

Open the dark robe from around my body

let it cut the mists

right through me.

Last night, my soul left the body

the way a breath exits a hot mouth

on a freezing day.

I go on opening

as the roof is dripping—

my shelter is melting

alongside the frost—

I am thawing apart.

The Sun is rising now

to end sleep.

This is the way the song-bird

wakes to its own music—

I don't know if a tree falls asleep.

But they do

dream.

And when a whole forest is dreaming

without doubt, full

of wonder,

it comes up

like the Moon.

And when all that dreaming thought

is carried into one sincere

vision of growing

for the expansion of each limb

and root of the woods—

that's when

    the Sun starts rising!

I wish to be there

when it does.

The Sun shines

on participation.

Sometimes

by way of the Moon,

so don't go rushing to bed!

This day is stirred

well awake.

    Here I am

still wearing last night's candle like a moth.

Time to open the shawl of the Mind—

clean my eyes.

Walk into the Day and the Moon

with new-born

Vision.

As Moisture is with the Night

This smoky room hides

a lovely presence.

A treasure inside a chest

you can't reach into

or unfold

with your hands.

Dusty wood flooring and the eye of a screw—

but look deeper:

a Taj Mahal stands within

the creasing of these wood grains.

Choose any old knot in the floor

and walk through the gateway

into Egypt's ancient secrets.

There is kindling beside the wood-stove—

just wait!

when our Friend comes

it will bud and bloom

into the wonderful gardens

of Babylonia.

This heart-clock knows

the Sun is slipping

to the other side of the cup.

    Soon I will strike up a candle,

drink from that light

for evening.

The Guest will arrive

with the strength of the turning Earth.

    Out here, in the living

of slow forces

and powerful majesty,

the dinner party is humble

but we cut our vegetables like warriors!

I open the doors

to invite in the Presence.

It arrives

right in time.

When that lord leaves his shoes at the entrance

it is the sky turning

gold, auburn,

and then red.

A moon from another world

drips off the candle stick.

This head, this pouring over the pen,

all these hand-written poems… bow,

a simpler man.

I still have not yet become

that full breath of a Man,

I am, still

young in my time.

Nonetheless,

this life is a Temple,

these words Prasad,

and days such as this,

communion, a precious

blending,

when I become with the Presence

as moisture is

with the Night.

Morning Mind

This morning mind

is a morning star,

the final one washed

by sunrise.

Wake early

to see this dawn-jewel

observing

the world stir softly

around this time when morning

is touching with the night.

Notice

its path above us

does not turn back

as this side

of Earth's face

slides away from her pillow.

Sleeping minds

develop

our dreaming days—

they can hardly conceive

of that point of brightness

which does not swerve

from this, it's final pleasure—

to be washed out,

absorbed,

into the great blue

Heart, at long last,

forever.

Mountain Truth

The shape of Truth-lips

are mountains to me.

The figure of a palm

cups a fresh lake

in my body.

    My Wonder-eye is raised

when the sky leads me on

like a road.

    Temped nights

inside the candle of aloneness

has shown where moonbeams touch

at the bottom of the pool—

what blows

through the drapes

of a sitting house.

    If this course of unfolding

pervades,

    perhaps great stones

will turn over

and begin creating art.

Perhaps the seeds of a color

never before seen

will be uncovered

out of a seam in the Earth.

I feel my Heart

in procession

with my feet and hands.

In partnership

like the Sun and

the Earth.

    When my tongue

and my convictions

are married

like the cranberry

and the root,

Then

have I begun

kissing the great ranges

of Truth-lips.

Breakfast in Eden

A pair of teeth

Sink into an apple.

Love is made there

Between the tongue

And fruit.

When your breakfast table

Is the surface -touch

Between the sea

And morning sky,

You will Dream

Like the gods.

Your shawl brushes my arm

When you pass—

A curtain of rain passes also

in the distance.

I am brought to stillness.

Moments like this remind me

To relax.

I know the Way

As the sprout knew

The way out of the seed.

A set of teeth

Sink into an apple

Like a bunch of children

Loving the Earth.

When your breakfast table

Is between the embracing

Of your Heart

And Heaven,

You will Love

Like the gods.

This Gratitude

I feel a gratitude

that skims poorness

and worry off my heart.

To see this sandalwood body

burning in the temple of the Earth,

I am thankful.

Use these moments well

when we see how far

along the wick our flame has come.

The past is not returnable.

Last night's candle-light is now beyond

you and the courtships,

the hateships,

of your memory.

Those seeds are already cast—

we are raining over them.

We are opened soil—

mouths that want to be kissed.

This gratitude comes to me

the way wheat-fields are nourished

and sprout from the Earth—

a long and new season,

tall grasses, hawks grazing,

and these strong strokes of wind

to measure me.

Father's House, Mother's Country

It is a far and flooded road

to the doorstep

of the Father's house.

Rain on rain

this stone in my heel

and a sun-beaten hat after

that lifetime spent in the fields—

these conditions in my mind

feel hardly suitable to weather

this mountain-hearted country.

However, my Soul

is five million years to the day

when I was an unconscious sleeper

in dust bowls

and gas plumes, in great space

still looking

for my Father's house.

I was once smoke

filling this good house

when the Earth was

still bleeding from birth.

It is true

a woman must be on Fire

before her breasts are full

with motherhood.

We become Love

bearing children by

becoming children ourselves.

And every man

who calls himself Her lover

or Her son

must work enflamed

with muscle and conviction

in that old wilderness,

again weaving the grassroots

of his Heart

into Her's.

A lamp swings in the window

of the Father's house.

I am a soft moth braving

hard nights out of the womb,

wandering for Light through the wild

of my Mother's country.

Facing the Wilderness of Beauty

A Man loves a beautiful face—

and now he has seen God's great work.

This drives him.

He builds a shelter deep

inside the moan of his Heartlands.

    Pits himself against winters

that do not bring laughter.

    Like the Mountains themselves,

he holds a hundred thousand

tons of snow on his back,

braving wild animals

with shoulders standing

nearly taller

than his courage.

    Fire upon

    fire

upon fire,

he gathers bush wood,

burning his way

through the harsh season.

    He endures this suffering

because he has seen

his Lord's great work.

    Every kind of weather will arise in him.

He becomes intimately familiar

with his austere shelter,

this unique form

rattling in the face of his Nature.

    His body is lean,

it is cold, it is warm,

it cries for hunger,

it bruises itself—

runs hard

like a deer

chased by a spirit-wolf.

He weeps

and the river charges toward

the borderless ocean.

Jesus was walking on those waters

when he went into the wilderness

to bear the labor pains of his Devil.

He saw the works of Beauty,

and his devotion to that

swung him in the fire

as a hammer of his Lord

to bend the course of Time.

A root within his Wisdom

pierced through the Temple floor

within him.

And even in the burning of torment

Jesus was washing the feet

of the untouchables—

he surrendered

everything.

His deer-body

stopped running.

    Gave himself totally

to the wolves of God's work

so he might be returned swiftly

to the Divine Emperor

who was out hunting Heart-game.

    Enter into that deep wilderness

to do the work that bends light

into a permanent season of beauty.

    Build a fire of remembering

every night

to keep you alive

in the fears of death.

    Walk into the wilderness

because you have seen the face of the Lord

and now you know

no other way.

Light and Shadow of the Stone

We are indeed our own difficulties.

The Light

and the Shadow

of the Stone.

With a Word

we move the mountain

from here

    to there.

But now it squats

directly in our path.

Such is

the paradox of our minds.

A Dove on a Stone

Walk up through the wide valley pass

and leave again through the narrow door.

Take to lighting up my Heart, brilliantly,

so I can move beyond mere believing.

The crows have the dove

pinned against the river's edge—

Does it sink in the charging water

or get taken apart by beaks?

This is when we learn to swim,

when someone who cares

throws a stone at our demons.

This is when Jesus came to Mary Magdalene

and wrote the Truth in the hot-sands

which burned her— which saved her.

This is when the Buddha

made the disciple weep flowers

of desperateness, surrendering him

to Enlightenment.

Cold winds come

to clear the flies

away from the lamp.

I am a dove

sitting on a stone.

A Season's Touch

You touched me

the way Autumn knows the garlic.

The trees bow in color

at your arrival.

Bonfire summer fades down.

Our deepest yearning

turns the pages of seasons.

    We write a new song

on a weeping mandolin.

The cello groans

for a new bow,

the lover comes

and releases its sadness.

You come to eat with me,

the end of the vegetables

before winter.

I pull a wool blanket

over the drum.

God will now

fill this land with snow.

Touch me that way again.

Mother Sighs

I wrap myself another time

in a deep blanket, for the warmth,

for the Heart of our Mother.

Because I feel from the Earth

a shivering sigh

coming to turn over my people.

Mother—You, who gave us.

Forever we are the white hairs

trembling upon your chin.

    I am only one

in the river flowing from your lips

which drools the blood of your children.

    Rays of sun

glance the oils of your cheek,

I shine also

pierced by your love.

    But I am only one

of many

who have gathered at the pit of your throat

listening for life's true meaning.

Mother— You, who ends us.

We do not mean to suffer so fearfully.

We do not mean our windless words

and airless loves,

for we cannot see clearly

that the collapse of our lungs

will be also

the fall of our Empires.

We are not seeing

that you fill us with the sky

with each breath.

That you fill us with life

in this very moment—

Yet we fear Death.

So I wrap myself another time

in a deep blanket, for the warmth,

for the Heart of our Mother

whose sigh will be the season

coming turn over my people.

Coupling Wilds

We love

what love comes deeply.

We blush, what secrets

come beating.

We rise together, sleepily.

This way the we aim

our quivering staffs—

is a mystery to my mind.

I care for you and I doubt you.

I love you and I fuck you.

Two wolves plunder

the same shining Elk.

Desire gleans like an oil-rich pelt.

The meat of our loving

frees open the bedroom door.

A white sheet has been pulled over

two moons— one the light of blueness,

the other, fire.

We are both feeling what magnifies

there, in the coupling of wilds,

as a fine atmosphere of the Heart

is wrapped further into us,

and further,

and still, further.

Wilding

I've become an aching, naked root

devoted to this undefined effort,

working through these fear-teeth

facing me out the wilding

of some Great Spirit.

Hearing this body cry out,

barren island

raped stone by the sea.

A mind dies

a clotted cave's root

full of darkness.

    Spirit makes up the difference.

Gradually sending, loving winds,

waves of passionate weather,

and these bathing changes of light,

wearing on

grinding the soil out of pain.

Rain on

rain on

rain,

begins sprouting the loving.

The earth-heart forgives,

reaches in

deeper

and begins wilding!

What was once fear

has become a tiger

in the eyes of a daughter

who loves you.

What was once an unbearable

Spirit, is a Wife

who takes you by the hand

into her wilderness of Beauties

and tenderly

devours us.

White Waters of Laughter

Deadness roles out

on these white waters

of laughter.

The Man crows at her early snow—

The Woman fills with milk, coming to the season

he lowers over her nature.

He enters her

and unfolds leaves, one

by one.

They couple like butter and fire.

She tangles into him—

She is the shower in his hair.

Soon, they unravel,

blankets shucked off the bed

loose wings of paper

falling autumn emotion.

They remain apart, until

the Man sees the Woman,

her eyes from afar,

and once again

they rush together!

Souls couple like leaves against

a wet window.

Where do I see them again?

Tumbling apart,

pebbles washed out

 by their own rain...

Lovers always stay near

to the energy that gives life.

So near

in heart-thoughts, yet still

assorted by so many earth-cloths,

these wet and endless soils

for working—

This cycle will continue

when we see You again,

let the deadness roll out,

here, on our white waters

of laughter.

Heaven and Morning

The clouds drift open

showing us the sky.

The Sun teases us

in the doorway of the bridal evening.

Breasts are the grass hills

tender are her pubic soils.

Humanity has married

to mill and sow their consciousness

into the Earth.

The deep fog joins us

here on the mountain

of revival.

The lightning may clap.

The thunder may pour.

It is no concern.

The drenching weather

cannot hoodwink

the children of devotion

for long.

The Sun creates a space for us

like a wife

in the garden.

Morning-time fills the windows

with silence.

The moaning of the night

was divided

by silence.

The opening of the closed

was hinged

on silence.

We penetrate dawn

until the flushed cheek of evening

rolls aside from us.

We absorb

into the night

where we observe our dreaming

trembling stars

from a mountain point.

The moment is pregnant.

The view

is heavenly.

This is our communion.

Heaven and Earth

sit together

holding hands.

Nature's children are conceived

by two bodies—

Silence

and   the Drum.

A Musical Conversation

Preface

A Musical Conversation—

I wandered outside this morning in the damp and inspiring winter fields, imbibed frost into my beard, a crow song on my ear drum, the gift of a tired muscle from the frozen ground. I walked to the coffee shop and saw people I love, sometimes fear... they remind me of where I stand in this human form. I sit down to write. Bringing insights from a sunrise-wilderness into this building, into these words. Interwoven into the crisp fibers of the paper in your book is the white frost sticking to a dormant cornfield, the snow that lingered on banks through a mountain pass— these are the subtle insights of ice melting. The spine of your book is the topic everyone in this coffee shop has come to talk about, to taste, to write, or to silently feel. It is winter, and memories of snow lie in meters of love upon the paper. Everything that goes into making me— makes you. It's not necessary that you become my friend, or even that you like me... the same music that governs like and dislike, personal and shared, is the same music spinning these little threads, You, and I.

We are all united in a deep musical way. We are connected to a mental jam-session that ignites us all in the fire of ideas. Our biorhythms tide like hips dancing all to the same moons, ebb and flow to the same colorful variations. We are all acting according to a musical conversation engaging our every heart, turning our minds into crescents and wholes, filling our bodies with aches and reliefs. We are interacting, regardless of how withdrawn one's own ego may appear to distance them— every song is singing.

There is something deeply personal to this universal music. Like a musician who puts special attention into each varying tone, so does the dynamic force of Life give attention, profound personality, into each and every player of the Universe. Seek out your tone, I encourage you. It will be as unique as starlings are from the peacock— as a chicken has particular work that is different and precious from those duties of an elk. This is not egoism. This is diversity. We are not the containments we put up to organize ourselves, these fences of identity— these buried stones of intellectual property. We are a one-mind jam— a constant and intimate musical conversation, somewhere between the rugged forms of Life and the softly piercing Presence of whatever we Love and behold, greater than ourselves.

Knat of Spirit

I am Spirit

cast into parcels

flung like an arrow from God's fingernail

like a knat I land, stuck

into this great dusty basin

of Life's oil.

Spirit dives into itself

as thirst

and the drinking—

fills itself with nourishing fat

and drowns.

Now, here I am.

Lost in it.

This oil might as well be wine—

I am so drunk

I forgot where I came from.

Being so bloated in oil

I think I am oil.

I forget Myself—

I sink deeper, again

and again.

My every effort

is frustrated,

yet,

a silent Knowing

never abandons Us.

Even as the oil

begins to roll, and I

am churning inside

riptides of myself,

somewhere deeper

in the quiet

subtle Knowing,

a Spirit is bathing

 in delight

and a voice whispers into the pot

containing me, gently

I hear it say,

"Keep on swimming."

Language

Existence once beached a song.

So, I am

sojourned from the Sea.

My growing Heart is one

lifting syllable.

My body

one dying nuance.

    I try to express this ocean

but then I wreck my tongue-ship.

    Just one moment ago

I was a vessel.

Now

I am debris.

    Such is the frustration

between language

and this vast, vast Song.

Folding Changes

You spoke a few invisible words inside

and now the earth is changing!

As if I am a disciple whose Master

instructed him to fold his robe

    one hundred new ways.

I am becoming a little more naked,

practicing my attentiveness

to these appearing shapes.

I fold, this way,

and a giant bird brings me to China.

I lay the crease, like this,

and India is pitched around me,

monsoons and temples.

    Like, that,

and I am surrounded

by a city tantrum.

If this corner is placed, here,

will Kashmir spread

like a carpet for my prayers?

Will Hong Kong roll a cigarette

and put it on my lip?

I dress myself with the robe again, and the way

it rests over my shoulders

is New Zealand in the morning

wearing dawn.

Touching these buttons,

each becomes the moon during the daytime

on a different day.

Leaving the Sanctuary to throw corn

to the chickens before meditation,

I see each kernel burst

into an American Great Plain.

Astonished,

I gaze at my palm

and flowing through it are the rivers Ganges,

and Kentucky.

Seeing a face I adore

walking up the path to meditation

the seams in my clothing fray.

I undress myself with my eyes.

Now I'm back where I started

naked as I came.

Maybe the master was trying to show

how the Soul has many shapes

and can fold to wear Itself

in so many

unique ways...

Sunrise Musical

Waking up late in the morning

after the sun has already risen

is a belated arrival

to the musical.

You've missed the foreplay

for the whole day.

The crescendo peak

may now come blankly.

You may not get-it

why the audience

is loving so deeply

with their eyes.

You may not feel

the tension in every instrument,

the compassion which

fingers every note.

Your old knees will lift you

to applause

instead of the Ovation

flying your heart out of your seat

like roses cast on stage.

Love is the auditorium,

the roof and the rain

a partnership.

Some will get wet in the weather.

Others will cross the parking lot

dancing their way

through the high waters.

At the Heart of Matter

A poem of the Heart,

a deep glistening root

is returning nutrients

into light.

Not with words.

We can't get there

this way.

You will have to strip away your shoes

and dance over me.

Every poem written

all Art

will have to forsake the tongues

that delivered them

and blossom together

like tulips in one

open field.

The earing and the grape

must reconcile their differences

and see

they both ornament

the same face.

Every mineral that travels

by way of this root

can see beyond the dark ground.

Regardless of blossom color

nut shape,

or crust of the bark,

there is an essence

at the heart of matter

full of the longing

to return.

Giving Medicine

A spoon comes to my lips.

Prayer is the way

I have to receive this medicine.

Prayer is the way

of a pine forest

amongst all other things—

In return for filling the land

with its shade

and open-armed

waves of fragrance,

it is given in return

its own glorious growing.

Prayer is mutual.

Not begging.

If you need from Life,

if you desire,

you need only

that within your very

scent and shadow

is the asking.

An act of true Giving

is not the package of the form

or time of delivery,

nor the lovely set of teacups

you unfold from inside.

The ugliness of the design

on the scarf

is irrelevant

when it is warming you

from the ice-biting air.

Inside your coughing,

within the fever-heat

in your mind,

you asked for it.

The medicine will come.

The form and arrival

is medicinal,

not ideal.

Be aware

of your wishing.

No song

or rebuking

can stop, once begun,

the purifying burn

 of fires sweeping our Hearts,

struck out of Life's

generous

Giving.

Sea-Foam

These thought-forms

creating our lives

are sea-foam,

gathered in the rolling white beards

of endless waves.

They go on and on,

developing

evolving

dissolving—

frothing in the sea

of formations.

Ego is not an island, my friends—

it is the driftwood floating nonsense

of all

we think

we know—

and our attitudes often

become our lame paddle.

Let go

of the ropes

holding you to this fear-boat.

Outlook

deep into the full night

of a conscious moon.

Observe out there

great whales of existence

who turn their dreams into song.

Submerged for lifetimes

learn from them the art

of diving deeper,

sustaining one's Self

on one breath of air.

We plunge into exploration

where light may not enter,

where creatures evolve to see

through their blindness.

Where we may conquer our fears

and bear the silence,

for our precious

awe inspired

insights

into

Being.

Myth of the Owl whose Shadow Touched the Moon

"How did the Owl who crossed the night

cast his shadow

on the Moon?"

There is a story about it...

There was once an Owl

who inherited the Majesty

of the Love Emperor—

to launch from that arm

meant the Sun brought itself down

to fold itself into his wings.

—You see

the Moon use to think of the Emperor so much

it immersed into love

by the mere passing

of His beautiful fowl.

The whole world of People use to step outside

in unison, and turn on!

Raise their lamps

and jars of fireflies

to witness the Emperor's wisdom-bird

crossing the night-sea.

Churning the butter

of each other's light

it was a communing for a single wish

to expose the flight patterns

of this ancient journey—

The Owl's shadow

would be cast up by the community

across the whole night of phenomena

and touch the Moon.

This sacred ritual use to be

brighter

than comprehension.

But the People soon forgot this mystery.

So a new story had to be told, for remembering:

There was an evening in Autumn

    when a terribly powerful King

called up every pair of arms

who could arc a bow in the Kingdom.

Every arrow in his nation was spent

on that sleepless night.

Each dipped in oil

and white fire

he launched everything they had, all at once,

on a gamble

to overtake the mystical fowl

with an overwhelming assault

for everlasting life—

    However,

no self-superior missile

can reach Heaven in that way.

The events contained a twist...

By lighting up the sky like that

he gave to the Owl a shadow

that could reach the Moon.

The King did not help himself—

The Heart Emperor, instead,

turned the actions around

to serve the hopeless of this world,

giving vibrancy to a myth

which pointed toward something timeless.

A story with the range

of a mythical event, meant

every person would have a chance

to hear the tale—

to remember within themselves

the Owl of Self-Knowing

and how the shadow from that light

can miraculously touch

the Moon.

Childhood in the Forest

Adults are always trying

to be adults.

    They Believe a Mystical Forest could exist— as a concept.

But too often we find them settling down into knots

tangled into the first branch of Philosophy.

    This Forest I speak of

is full of Children.

They hang from the vegetation

like after a fresh rain.

    Sensible adults who wander

into here, looking for revenue,

have their fine-crafted faces dismantled—

because these Children think and move

under the same influence

a water droplet rolls to plunge

from a leaf.

A rational man

with a sophisticated sense for research

and citations,

starts talking to the Children about

the dense equations of Enlightenment,

references to highly evolved discourses

and hardily composed theorems

of the Self—

He went on and on about this stuff...

Adults are always trying to be Adults.

The children

they looked at each other

and transformed into a herd of deer

running into the light cast

through the trees.

    A child is far too clear

for that kind of talk.

Adults come through here

slapping on drums with

sticks and bones,

painfully out of rhythm,

proclaiming:

"I am a Ghanaian Percussion Master!"

    Then,

Spirit blows through

shaking the Children's

tambourine hearts.

    Every tree becomes

a flute-cane,

black branches of sugar music,

accompanied by swaying choirs

of bamboo

crowded with birds.

Light hairs are crafted into brooms

for shaking those majestic, colored intonations

brighter from the autumn leaves.

For sweeping away

any brittle   *thinking*

about love.

Once upon a time,

      a mighty paper castle

came crashing out of the clouds

into this Forest...

Snapping, splintering tree-limbs,

smoke swelling,

casting a huge sound, plunging

into the river, throwing

waves over the shore,

this architecture of vast wealth

had just been razed to heaven.

When the commotion settled,

Children came and found a man

walking from the wreckage, weeping

and on fire with suffering.

    "What's wrong?" the Children asked.

"It all came down in a storm," said the man.

"I have lost everything.

All that I am is

there, washing away in the river—

I have become nothing— nobody!"

    One of the children giggled:

"That wasn't a storm....

"That was the Spirit

in the form of monsoon season.

You have survived a blessing."—

Another child playfully spoke,

"You will sit under these trees

and laugh yourself

to death

at this divine joke, one day."

Remain in the forest long enough

and you will surely

kneel at the river to drink.

Close your eyes

look inward you see

the tons of leaves and water

which fall here passing

upon us in all their fullness,

reminders to us all

of unconquerable

Change.

If you do begin to see, You too

 will drop yourself into the river

one stone   at a time.

Buddha Moon

You have come to visit

this sleeping palace

like the whispering footprints

of a deer in the garden.

If sleep was not my obsession

I could wholly adore

your white dreams

through the window.

Yet I am

asleep.

Pilgrim of the stars

there is a cast of smiling shadows

around your conversations of light.

You're always moving

silent

in meditation on the Sun.

Could you rise this dawn

behind my closed eyes of mind?

Teach to me the art

of awakening

with Heart.

Beloved Coming

My beloved,

should you ever come to me

where my head lies unconsciously,

would you be there

shining and melting

like morning through the bedroom window?

If you should come

here to the bar of the brimming wine-hearts,

you find me drunk as stars

and you say aloud, "Drink and Shine!"

Should you come

when I am fighting silence in the Garden

you ask me

to listen

the way soil takes in the rain.

Should you come to me

when I am hiding

like a teenager refusing to get out of bed,

you say, the way a lover might say,

"wake up, dear one,

there's no use pretending."

Should you come to me

when I shiver far apart

from myself.

You unravel your robe

and speak with body-heat,

"I see you."

Should you come to enter

the tipsy burlesque of my mind,

fill my arms with a coat and hat,

and say

"There is snow outside on the Temple—

come and see!"

Should you come

to this shy corner of my bedroom

you kneel and say to me

"let us pray in the way

a candle burns."

Should you come to me,

beloved one,

when in ignorance

I have taken sides opposite

of our love,

you say nothing

but gaze at me like the moon

stares at the world.

Winter Temple

A Season changes the Tree

as Winter settles our feet.

    As the frost takes our gardens,

so our rice begins to swell—

passions turned to sleep

soils burdened by cold.

Like a cup of tea

will our Hearts soften

and warm us,

    while prayer is the candle flame

to soothe the solitude.

Remembering our devotion

baptized by a bhakti sun,

we truly learn to become

disciples

who melt like snow.

Longing I have Lost the Moon

I find myself

searching so longingly.

I have lost the Moon.

I am seeking so far

for the milk of that sky.

Am I led astray?

With sadness on nights that tear the cloth

I wonder if there exists a rope—

a rope to lead my caravan

through the capes of this great shadow

cast by such a great light...

This separation

is as thick as an

almond's skin.

Yet I heard my soul cry-out

like a horse lost in the foothills.

I close the window, hopelessly.

the breeze was reminding me

of a story—

Long ago, In a dusty village,

near a humble boondocks mosque,

I wandered upon another man's heart,

beside him was his lover's,

staked outside a garden wall

as if they wished to say

"Our baths are filled with Love

in here!"

I felt the wind blowing that day

and wondered, cynically, if slowly

it would steal away

with their beating young love—

if it would leave them standing

beside each other

as Strangers.

I shrugged off my contemplation

and continued filling my mind

with dreaming

of the Godhead—

It was then, I heard,

air-songs of playful love-making

coming from behind the flower bushes

as I walked away...

That burning intimacy

filled me

with the longing

even more...

Somewhere I have lost the Moon.

I open the window again

to see if it is outside.

The fresh air

was a kind of remembering.

It was then I saw, the Divine Lion, dancing in the distance

with a cool fire of laughter.

His Grace was a type of hunting

for your deepest heart-thoughts.

His movements along the blue streak

of dawn, spun the stone-beds around him

into dreaming about

the pins and needles of loving.

Inside my chest the sky folded down, bowing

to that beautiful night-face.

There was a star-standing ovation

that will die clapping.

Here lies a side of the Moon

the world never sees.

Likewise there is a side to my Mind

only the Mystery

has the angle to reveal.

Longingly, I have lost the Moon.

I clasp my cloak together

with a pin made of soul-water

and guide my longing out the door

to continue the journey

holding the inspiration within,

in a perfect water-bag

like the Moon.

Egg and Sky

Handle this

gently I pray to you.

This heart is an unbroken egg, perfectly

the Sun does not drip away.

Walk towards it, approach

as you would a Wonder,

a Majesty that commands our eyes

to sacrifice sight

back into the sky of awe.

Gardens are there

which do not grow up

nor in.

No conversation ever

took place, asking

about rightness

or wrongdoing—

no guilt soil

no rejected fruit.

We feed our hunger

with hunger

until our yield is desperately full.

    Then something divine walks

into us for harvest.

Then your Soul

gasps

at my Soul.

Then my Heart

moans

with your Heart.

Then the egg is broken.

You and I,

Us and They,

World and Earth,

equally yoked

as a breath is mingled

with the sky.

What is Inside

What is Inside us

comes into form

as Life.

    Musicians come to visit this poet

opening their musical boxes

as he himself

is becoming an instrument.

    This poet turns over in his sleep

from a heart-aching question

he dreamt.

    So someone who loves him

 rolls out of his bed

to spread the blinds

to a morning of answers.

It all begins Within.

Temple

Kneel to pray

the way

a tiger by himself

leans over a lakeside to drink.

Completely natural, with a thirst

more powerful

than the animal.

Not a religious creation.

Be genuine

and heart messages will be sent

like the time the jasmine

flowers caught fire, and then the winds came.

Now those blossom-embers

blow through my library

bringing it down in flames,

all because I asked

"How do I get out of here?"

The Earth and Consciousness

longed for Union

so long, until they made together

Temples to walk in the lands and love.

We need no other building

for that purpose

but Our Selves.

Develop the courage to be

like the sweet apple who merged

with the lean deer. Transformed

into its grace, forsook

the orderly rows of the orchards

to experience the wider connection

of valley roaming

and watering foothills.

Be brave

and tear away the Robes,

the Books.

Swing open your own window

inside the Temple of Faith.

Musical Conversation

A musical chord strikes out of the night

by the sound of lovers

two reeds in white sheets

speaking with musical conversation.

A visionary musician becomes enchanted

into the practice of his Art.

He sits deeply in the moonlight

and loses himself

 to it All.

The stars are in Kirtan

with the Moon.

That musician forgot himself

into the Names

chanted by that Sky.

A Woman who felt the love stir within her

stretched her soul across her hollow body

to become a drum

for the hands of the Earth.

A musical chord strikes out of the wilderness

by the sound of the warrior

breaking his bow on the shot

for that white Elk of his Soul.

Hearts as clear as singing-bowls

come walking out of that forest

from time to time.

Meanwhile the world of heavy hearts

crowd into the Tavern

with live music.

They hear the reed-music

playing on the roof.

That musician from the forest

who plowed a wooden root from his Mind

and carved it into a love-singing flute.

That musician who struck his own mighty chord

now surrenders himself to a constant

ongoing

musical conversation

with the Sky.

From a Mountain

One year and a half on the Mountain, in the shade of Sadhana

and good works, breaking bread.

I have loved.

Yes, it exists

as something deeper

than your lips.

It was always there, behind

the conversation.

Inside

the madness, like a coy fish

concealed in the algae and the lilies.

Now, friends,

a wave has brought me down

to the roads of men

and chattering lights

of the World

Am I Enlightened?

As Enlightened

as the leg

of a throne.

Am I liberated?

As free

as a finger

pointing to the stars.

Where will I go now?

Well,

I won't sit on the floor

like a rock.

This stone has been shaped now

into a wheel.

 Life's caravan moves towards Heaven's Cities,

and some loving Souls

and gentle Teachers

have tied my rope to the hitch

of this ancient

moving journey.

Secrets in Forests

There is a leaf stuck on my cheek

engraved with a password

into Life's rejoicing trove

of Secrets.

    A stone remains in my boot

while I learn its painful lesson.

    There are holy men who have taken away their shoes

for the Temple is flooding regularly

with a divine Presence.

    A Star has come down to your beautiful lips

like an herb from your last meal.

    I see this and realize

You are a Full being.

    Yet in some way

still always thirsty.

Something always nursing

from behind the cup of your skin.

We come to learn how to trust

our bodies to the raining aloes

of these Spiritual Forests.

Yet we must also remember,

    and remember well,

that a Marble floor is no place

for a fresh loaf of bread.

Just the same

the cutting board is no place for a stone.

    Some people break into intricate tombs

finding rooms full of salt

when they were out looking for The Secret.

    But there is no ancient artifact

with a historical salvation

for us today.

    The secret is already rolling in the mountain stream.

We learn how to love

from the drinking deer—

we learn how to listen

from deep within.

    You can catch a firefly

or you can catch a wasp—

either way

we need to test our ability

against something,

whether it teaches us how to let go,

or gives to us a little light

of wonderment.

    It is a worthwhile life

searching these unseen forests inside us

for that single bird's nest

where a precious secret

is silently hatching.

Spring Cleaning

A seed was buried into the earth

under a ground-blanket—

wait and watch

how its longing grows.

    Visit the maturing orchards

without shoes—

the grass is covered in people

hung with new blossoms.

It is still early.

They are showing their beauty-pedals

like children sent outside to play

and test their new muscles.

Butterflies open

and close on the garden walls.

A young man brings chai to the table.

Someone spontaneously

starts singing.

    Any moment

after this song

this place will get busy with work

as if the crowd stood up

for applause.

Spring cleaning.

The harvest will be coming

like the banners of an honored Emperor.

Everything will be swept and tidied.

Baskets repaired.

Rice must be cleaned.

Lunch is being prepared

for everyone.

Soon summer arrives

full of birds and ripeness,

melting our ambitions

with afternoon heat.

"Give yourself to this loving," it will say.

I will say,

"Help me flow like water through your hair."

It's Raining Outside and Life, is Beautiful

We are living, my Friends!

   Our Hearts bear apples, pears.

Hazelnuts connect each morning with the mango.

The peach kisses the wheat pastures.

The whole-meal burns with the salt flats

and the sugar cane.

I watch you wrap a basil leaf

around a cherry tomato

and I think of loving.

We may all become drunks,

wine-fools kissing

the roots of this grapevine.

We may become confused,

hording and trading the grape leaf,

wrapping ourselves up in it,

forgetting the aroma of laughter

we first fell in love with.

Life does not seem to regret

as we often do

the ways we have cried out in hunger.

We go astray— it happens.

Break an oath

or break a heart,

yet we come again to remember

that we are Alive, my Friends,

and this is the empowering truth.

Please, dear ones, let us not

complicate the situation of our loving.

Enter into me,

the way a deer meanders into the summer

field of sweet peas.

Bring your fresh tea leaves,

those gentle thoughts.

Bring the wholegrain of your body,

in your nakedness I see

the shapes of a thousand different seeds.

Bring the mold-wine of your desires,

I will bring my empty cups,

all that is in me

that holds you—

these many bowls of joy.

Come, my Friends,

it is raining outside and Life, is beautiful.

Come again,

    and again,

feast on that truth with me.

I would like to express gratitude to Anahata Yoga Retreat and the Seva crew who was present at the time, for opening up your home and insights, and offering a place and a means for doing the good-work within myself.

I would like to thank Swami Mukti Dharma, for sharing tools of wisdom with me, for taking me into your experiment, and for knowing who I am, especially when I couldn't see.

I want to thank Shantachittam, for your encouragement, for your listening, for asking questions, and for your loving support, without which, so many cupboards in my Heart would have remained closed ... I would not be the man I am today.

Thank you Brandon, for the countless smoke-breaks that continue to stretch my mind deeper into brotherhood. For being a witness to me, my work, and my growth into becoming human. Thank you for your gregarious hints into the heart, over all these years.

And thank you, Young Smith, for seeing (and voicing) the potential that was in me for writing, and also clearly marking where I still needed work. Thank you for the many classes I attended and the insights you offered to a young and ambitious poet.

Thank you to everyone who has played their role. Your fire is in this Book.

Note~

I wrote the Poetry in this collection out of devotion, to myself and a relationship I needed to express.

The Book, however, I have published for You.

Should you have anything you'd like to say, or share, reach me at:

rhapsodyofart@gmail.com

You can find more writings and projects from Joseph Montgomery at:

www.rhapsodyofart.com

Made in the USA
Charleston, SC
20 November 2014